GOD SPEAKS TO
LIBERIANS
AT HOME AND ABROAD

GOD SPEAKS TO
LIBERIANS
AT HOME AND ABROAD

A CALL ON LIBERIANS TO PRIORTIZE COVENANT
FAITHFULNESS TO GOD, RECONCILIATION,
REBUILDING AND GOOD STEWARDSHIP

Gehleigbe Bobson Bleh

authorHOUSE®

AuthorHouse™
1663 Liberty Drive
Bloomington, IN 47403
www.authorhouse.com
Phone: 1-800-839-8640

Published by AuthorHouse   09/12/2012

ISBN: 978-1-4678-8391-7 (sc)
ISBN: 978-1-4678-8392-4 (e)

DEDICATION

This Book is dedicated

- ❖ To the Almighty God who has spared my life and given me the wisdom and knowledge to write.

- ❖ To the loving memory of Martha Biah Bleh, the wife of my youth and partner in ministry. Death snatched her out of my hands during child birth on July 13, 2000! She encouraged me when I shared with her my plan to write this book and she even read the first manuscript. May her soul rest in perfect peace!

- ❖ To the Memory of Carolyn Thomas of Texas, USA, a good friend and supporter of my family and ministry.

And

- ❖ To My wife Susannah and Children, Marthalene Kou-Walakewon, Thalee Sue Grace, Caroline Lorkeah, Aaron, Miriam, Lucretia and all the children of Liberia. Jesus loves you!

CONTENTS

for me and my family. Rev. Dennis and Georgia Alstott are my spiritual parents, who sponsored me in seminary and with their prayers and support prepared me to be minister. Sis Carolyn Thomas (deceased) and her husband Merle Thomas of First United Methodist Church, San Augustine, TX, USA, are also great inspirations and supporters of our ministry and family. She is now with the Lord. She was a generous and concerned friend to my family. We named our daughter Caroline in memory of her. Mrs. Carolyn Ladner and the Mission Committee of the First United Methodist Church of San Augustine, Texas, USA, today continue to support my family and ministry. The Mission Committee sponsored my graduate study which earned me a Master's degree. It is worthy to make mention of Dr. Vicki Kloosterhouse, the Dean of the College of Education, ABC University, Yekepa, Liberia, who did a great job on my book. She took her time to do the editing and provided me meaningful advices.

❖ You are all wonderful people plus countless friends including Rev. Augustus D. Kings, Pastor Franklin Larmie, and Michael W. Torpor, II. Most importantly, My Love, Susannah who spared me time to be by myself to do the book project. I love you! Finally, to the editorial staff who completed the work. God bless you!

FOREWORD TO GOD SPEAKS TO LIBERIANS AT HOME AND ABROAD

It has been said, and quit rightly too, that there are no winners in war, only losers. This saying is being exemplified in the very tragic Liberian war, for no matter the situation in that once peaceful and "Christian" country before the war the events and consequences of that war made the pre-war situation pale into insignificance. Who won that war? The objective answer is nobody. Who suffered and is suffering? Liberians primarily and West Africa by extension.

One of the lessons of war is that the painful memories never end, and vengeance, no matter how just cannot eradicate the consequences. If anything at all, it prolongs it.

ACKNOWLEDGEMENT

The writing of this book would not have been a reality without the team effort of Professor Christian Adjei, former President of Ghana Christian University (formerly Ghana Christian College and Seminary), who wrote an inspiring foreword to this book. He has always been a good advisor to Liberians. All my former professors, especially Professor Manual Adjei, who taught me Old Testament History and Biblical Prophets and Miss Dorothy Enuson, Professor of Christian Education.

❖ I want to mention Sister Layson Zuu, former youth president of Miller McAllister UMC Ganta, who copied my draft for typing the complete manuscript. Nana Akua Opoku of First Choice Communication Center, Accra, Ghana, did the first typesetting of the manuscript and permitted me to edit it.

❖ My spiritual leader, the Resident Bishop of The Liberia Annual Conference, Rev. Dr. John G. Innis, who read the manuscript and encouraged me to publish it.

❖ I do not want to forget about my secret giants, specifically, Rev. and Mrs. Herbert S. L. Zigbuo, my foster parents who sponsored my education from High School through college. Mrs. Sue W. Milwee, my former Algebra Teacher at Ganta United Methodist School also sponsored me in college and graduate school. She is indeed a sister in Christ, who continues to be a source of blessings

How then do we end this tragedy of tragedies in West Africa? Gheleigbe Bobson Bleh has sought to do it the way he knows how, God's way. Using the four prophetic oracles from the book of Haggai, Pastor Bleh, a trained minister of the Gospel urges Liberians to use the tested and never failed way, God's way.

In the Book of Isaiah 48:16-19 we read, "Come closer and listen. I have always told you plainly what would happen so you would have no trouble understanding. And now the Sovereign Lord and His Spirit have sent me with this message. The Lord your Redeemer, the Holy One of Israel (Liberia) says, I am the Lord your God who teaches you what is good and leads you along the paths you should follow, oh, that you had listened to my commands! Then you would have had peace flowing like Gentle River and righteousness rolling like waves. Then you would have become as numerous as the sands along the seashore—too many to count! There would have been no need for your destruction." (New Living Translation of the Holy Bible).

This book is worth reading and the advice worth implementing, for it carries the admonition of God who loves all Liberians. There is nothing to lose and all to gain.

Prof. Christian Pat Adjei
Former President, Ghana Christian University (formerly Ghana Christian College & Seminary) Accra, Ghana.

PREFACE

God Speaks to Liberians at Home and Abroad is the author's call to all Liberians to prioritize covenant faithfulness to God and the rebuilding of our nation through reconciliation, forgiveness and good stewardship that can lead to total freedom for all Liberians. In this book I differentiate between three sets of Liberians: those who stayed home, those who went abroad, and those who fled during the war. An understanding of how each group is defined will help in the reading of the book.

Liberians at home refers to all (politicians, civil servants, religious leaders, business people, farmers, community leaders, chiefs, elders, students, etc . . .) who never left the country from the beginning to the end of the war. Greed and the grab for power were the primary motivations for 14 years of a bloody and senseless war. The Liberians who stayed experienced every bit of the war, for they had nowhere to run. Thousands were killed in cold blood at the hand of wicked men and women who claimed to be liberators. Others refused to die outside their motherland and they cried, "It is better for me to die in my own country than to die in next men's country."

Liberians abroad refers to those Liberians who have left the country prior to the civil war for the purpose of education, economic prosperity or greener pastures, but failed to help develop Liberia. Some of these Liberians continue to denigrate their homeland.

Liberians forced to flee is the next group to which I will refer. They were forced to flee the country because of the war and found themselves in refugee camps around the world. These Liberians may have suffered the most devastation in that they lost their homes, properties, loved ones and freedom. Some of them have refused to return home; they feel that persons who harmed them during the war have not been brought to justice.

It is my prayer that as you read and reflect on the message of the Book of Haggai, you will take consolation in the word of God like the children of Israel, who lived in exile for 70 years. Finally, God called them to return home and begin to rebuild their nation. As we sit by our rivers of Babylon, we should remember Liberia, our Zion, and Sweet Land of liberty. We must work together to rebuild our nation to become what God has destined it to be.

The Book of Haggai has always been a source of strength for me as a young minister. My first contact with the book of Haggai was during the 1980's, when the late Evangelist Joseph Gonkpalah of the United Liberia Inland Church delivered a challenging sermon from it. I also studied Haggai under Prof. Manual Adjei as part of my course in Biblical Prophets. Then the Rev. Jakes S. Voker, former District Superintend of Gompa District of the United Methodist Church, scheduled me to do a Bible study at the 45th Session of the District Conference, which was held with the Jermu UMC in Central Liberia. During the three day study, many people were touched when the lesson was applied from a Liberian perspective. After numerous requests, I was moved by the Holy Spirit to write this book.

I started the writing project in 1998, I have continued to work on it and have revised some portions as things have unfolded in our country. May this book helps us to draw closer to God and become good instruments in rebuilding our country and our broken lives. Remember in spite of our backgrounds, we are one people, with one nation, one history, and one destiny. This book is not solely written for Liberians but all who want to live in obedience to God's Word that states, "Covenant faithfulness brings security and prosperity both individually and nationally."

The Book of Haggai is one of the Old Testament's books that have the shortest chapters. A fast reader will take about seven minutes to complete the reading of the whole book. However, the Bible should not be read like a newspaper, but should be read for understanding and application. The message of the book is very touching. It is relevant to every person's situation and nation, especially what we (Liberians) have experienced. As you go through the book you will read about people who have had the same experiences, hurts, histories etc . . . as ours. The Israelites had been chosen by God to lead a godly life. Instead, they chose to turn their back on God, which led to their own destruction. Liberians have a similar story. Our nation was founded on Christian principles. We were chosen by God to live out before others these Christian principles. The very principles that is able to bring light, hope and freedom to the dark continent of Africa, whose inhabitants are blinded with satanic worship, hatred, injustices and dehumanization by Africans as well as foreign powers. History proves that Liberia the first black Republic in Africa, fought for the independence of other African countries. However, we have left the godly principles laid down by our founding fathers and mothers and instead have enslaved ourselves to the evil we came to change. The consequences of our disobedience are the war, economic hardship and the suffering for our people today.

The book is styled in such a way that the readers are given the background, the scripture passages, the exposition of the scripture passages and the reflection on its message from a Liberian perspective.

The first chapter introduces you to the book and the background of the book of Haggai.

The second chapter, which is the first oracle tells how the prophet Haggai rebuked and challenged his people to review their actions and set up right priorities by rising up to rebuild the temple of God, the success of rebuilding their nation. Liberians are challenged in this chapter to set right priorities by pledging their allegiance to God and then to the rebuilding of our nation. Unless the Lord builds, its builders labor in vain (Psalm 127)

The third chapter discusses the second oracle when the people felt despair and apathy leaving the temple project. The prophet encouraged the people to gather hope and strength to continue the project. Similarly, many Liberians do not want to even associate with their fellow Liberians and reject being identified as a Liberian. These Liberians are ashamed of the horrible things their fellow Liberians continue to do in and outside of Liberia. The message is that God can change the situation around when we respect each other and stand as one people to rebuild a better Liberia.

Chapter four discusses the third oracle that describes the people's attitudes toward God. The Israelites were practicing all sort of evil vices and because of that God brought economic hardship upon them. Again, the prophet reminded them to prioritize holiness and give to the work of God. Like the Jews of Haggai's day, Liberians are involved in all sort of evil vices that have brought disgrace and curses upon our nation and us. We need to prioritize justice, peace, and love and live as God fearing, civilized people.

The fifth chapter, which is the fourth oracle, assured the Jews of God's vengeance upon wicked nations that humiliated Israel. Though the Jews sinned against their God, those nations that took them captive mistreated them and plundered their land, were not to go free. God promised to restore Israel and make it powerful like that of the kingdom of David. Liberians are called upon to forget about revenge because God will surely punish those who have committed atrocities against Liberians.

The book concludes with the message that Liberians have the consciences, strengths, and zeal to rebuild our country, but we need to prioritize God in our lives and in every national issue, knowing that sin brings reproach to any nation. We must unite and kick injustices, wickedness, tribalism, and war out of our country. By renouncing and resisting such practices, God can bring economic prosperity, security and peace to our land.

Finally, I believe there is a great need for healing and reconciliation among Liberians. In order to start the healing and reconciliation process appendices provide some helpful information on the step to peace and healing as well as son patriotic songs that would keep us in the spirit of unity.

CHAPTER ONE

Background To The
Study Of Haggai

To understand the book of Haggai, it first must be understood historically in the larger context of the Old Testament **relevant to God's plan for all ages**. Careful word study shows that the name Haggai means "festive of Jehovah" or "Joyous of Jehovah." It was a common name in Israel. Haggai, the prophet, might have lived in exile in Babylon. He was a committed patriot who sought to see the temple, their center of worship, rebuilt and worship restored. He also had courage to challenge his people to set the right priorities by turning to Jehovah God and living holy lives. In a space of four months, Haggai delivered four powerful oracles or messages from God rebuking, challenging and encouraging the returnees to remain committed to covenant faithfulness. He let them know that rebuilding the temple was a divine task from God and as such it much be obeyed at all times.[1]

The reading of the Old Testament, clearly demonstrates that we should not be surprised by the Israelites disobedience of God's covenant in Haggai. From the creation of mankind we see the consequences of God's children breaking covenant with Him. We also see the loving grace of God as He restores his people. To understand Haggai, we first have to understand the historical perspective of the Old Testament, which precedes the book of Haggai.

---

[1]   The Lion's Handbook to the bible, pp. 306-7.

The problem that led to the captivity of the children of Israel was because of covenant disobedience on their part disobedience of the covenant. Biblically God has been dealing with humankind more than any other creature made by Him from the time of creation up to present. When sin came into the world through Adam, it affected the complete human race. However, God raised Noah, the only righteous man of his generation in order to maintain the seed that would crush the head of the serpent (Genesis 3:15). God destroyed the wicked people by the flood and only seven other persons survived the flood. These people were to live faithfully and raise families, people and nations that would fear God and live in accordance with His eternal plan. Unfortunately, the flood did not destroy the sinful nature, which the Noah family inherited from Adam. Sin spread and deformed the human race. The human mind was no longer seeking God but fame and power. The Towel of Babel is a typical example of the attitude of Noah's generation. God being all knowing foresees man's plan against His plan for all ages. Consequently, God decided to use one of the sons of Noah, Shem so that He could fulfill the promise made to Adam and Eve. The lineage of Shem was maintained so that God could draw all humankind to Himself.

Unconditionally, God made covenant with one of the descendants of Shem, the man known in the Bible as Abraham. In the Genesis' account, God told Abraham that through him He would draw all humankind to Himself (Gen. 12:1-3). In other words, God was saying that the descendants of Abraham would be the medium through which all the people of the earth would know the living God. In order to implement the plan, God needed a centrally located place where He could multiply the decedents of Abraham; and mold their minds to live a righteous lifestyle that would influence others and drive out wickedness (Gen. 15:1-21). In view of the foregoing, God promised to give Abraham and his decedents the land from the River of Egypt (Nile) to the Great River Euphrates (the Persian Gulf). The inhabitants were very wicked and God was going to use the descendants of Abraham to punish them (Gen. 15:1-21). However, before that could happen, the descendants of Abraham were in slavery in Egypt for over four hundred years.

In His grace, God fulfilled His promise to Abraham when he miraculously delivered the children of Israel from Egypt. The Israelites spent forty years in the wilderness, renewed the covenant, captured the Promised Land

and were directly controlled by God (theocracy). Once again we see the pattern of disobedience unfold, as those who followed after Israel's great King David, sought other gods rather than Jehovah. Under the kingship of Solomon, idolatry entered the land of Israel thereby breaking covenant faithfulness with God. God vowed that the people would be punished for such a grave sin against Him.

During the kingship of Rehoboam, Israel divided into north and south (Israel and Judah). This sad incident came as a result of Rehoboam's foolish decision (1Kings 12:1-13). The Northern kingdom, which was led by Jeroboam, became very idolatrous, with Baal becoming their god. The Southern Kingdom, Judah, maintained the true worship of God, although they often fell in sin due to pressure from foreign powers. God through His prophets warned them many times that covenant disobedience would bring national disaster and insecurity, while faithfulness would bring security and prosperity both nationally and individually.

In 722 BC, God allowed the Assyrians to invade Israel and destroy all of its inhabitants and later in 558 BC to destroy Judah. The Babylonians destroyed Judah, with captives taken into exile in Babylon for 70 years. During this period of captivity, the Jews never forget about their God and continued to worship Him. God heard their cry and at the end of the 70 years period and raised another pagan leader, Cyrus of Persia, to free His people from the Babylonian captivity. Cyrus issued an edict permitting the Jews to return home to rebuild the temple of God and their home (Ezra 1:17). There were three stages of repatriation in line with Cyrus' edict. Zerubbabel led the first one as a governor appointed by Cyrus. This group built the altar and laid the foundation of the temple. The second repatriation was led by Ezra 80 years later (Ezra 7), and the third one was led by Nehemiah 13 years later. The success of the Jews aroused the Samaritans and other neighbors to oppose the rebuilding project and halted the work until Darius became the king of Persia in 522 BC. In the midst of the opposition, the Jews focused on their own building project. It was on this occasion that God sent Haggai and Zechariah to stir the people to continue the rebuilding project on the temple[2].

---

[2]   Manual Adjei's lecture notes Ghana Christian College and Seminary, 1996.3
       ibid

As you proceed with the reading of Haggai, you will discover in the first oracle some characteristics that are relevant to our time and experience. You will understand that in our rebuilding process, we need to first prioritized covenant faithfulness to our God. We must be faithful people who would put God first in all that we do in nation building.

CHAPTER TWO

The First Oracle:
The Call To Prioritize Rebuilding
The Temple And Covenant Faithfulness

READING THE SCRIPTURE: (HAGGAI 1:2-15)

1. *In the second year of DARIUS the king, on the first day of the sixth month, the word of the Lord came by the prophet Haggai to Zerubbabel the son of Shealtiel, governor of Judah, and to Joshua the son of Jehozadak, the high priest saying.*

2. *"Thus says the Lord of hosts," This people say, "The time has not come, even the time for the house of the Lord to be rebuilt."*

3. *Then the word of the Lord came by Haggai the prophet saying,*

4. *"Is it time for you yourselves to dwell in your Paneled houses while this house lies desolate?*

5. *Now therefore, thus says the Lord of host, "Consider your ways!*

6. *"You have sown much, but harvest little, you eat, but there not enough to be satisfied, you drink, but there is not enough to become drunk;*

you put on clothing, but no one is warm enough; and he who earns, earns wages to put into a purse with holes;

7. *Thus says the Lord of hosts, consider your ways!*

8. *"Go up to the mountains, bring wood and rebuild the temple that I may be pleased with it and be glorified", says the Lord.*

9. *"You look for much, but behold, it comes to little, when you bring it home, I below it away. Why?" declares the Lord of hosts, "Because of my house which lies desolate, while each of you runs to his own house.*

10. *Therefore, because of you the sky has withheld its dew, and the earth has withheld its produce.*

11. *"And I called for a drought on the land, on the mountains, on the grain, on the new win, on the oil, on what the ground produces on men on cattle, and on all the labor of your hands."*

12. *Then Zerubbabel the son of Shealtiel, and Joshua the son of Jehozadak, the high priest with all the remnant of the people, obeyed the voice of the Lord their God and the words of Haggai the prophet, as the Lord their God had sent him.*

13. *Then Haggai, the messenger of the Lord, spoke by the commission of the Lord to the people saying," I am with you, declares the Lord."*

14. *So the Lord stirred up the spirit of Zerubbabel the son of Shealtiel, governor of Judah, and the spirit of Joshua the son of Jehozadak, the high priest, and the spirit of all the remnant of the people, and they came and worked on the house of the Lord of host, their God,*

15. *On the twenty-fourth day of the sixth month in the second year of Darius the king.*

UNDERSTANDING THE SCRIPTURE

Haggai 1:1. One important thing Haggai does is that he dates his book. His message came in 520 B.C the second year of King Darius II of Persia. Darius had succeeded Cambyses (529-521 B.C)[4] who did not implement Cyrus's edict concerning the return of the Jews to their homeland to rebuild the temple of God in Jerusalem (Ezra 6:15). Throughout the book Haggai addresses Zerubbabel and Joshua the High Priest. Zerubbabel was a descendant of King David appointed by the Persian authority to lead the remnant. The reason is that these authorities could well dissimilate God's message to all the people. Meaning that Zerubbabel as governor would relate to the people on civil matters, and Joshua as the high priest would relate to the people on religious matters. By virtue of their positions, the people would adhere to them.

Haggai 1:2-11. In this section, Haggai states the problem God had with the people. The first group of returnees had come with zeal to rebuild the temple but the zeal soon died as a result of opposition from the occupants of the land (Ezra chapter 4). Apathy brought the temple to a standstill. Instead of persisting, they began to build paneled houses for themselves. In the midst of this opposition and apathy, God sent Haggai to stir them up. In his first oracle Haggai confronted the people telling them that they had forgotten their priority. Instead of the temple, which represented God's presence, they were building fine houses for themselves. He told them to examine their ways as to whether it was fair for them to live in paneled houses while God's house lies desolate. He helped the people to realize that agriculture and economic prosperity were withheld because they had not prioritized the Lord; but instead cherished less important things more than God himself. He admonished the people that agriculture and economic prosperity would return to the land when they resume the work on the temple.

Haggai 1:12-15. Within three weeks period, the message that came through prophet Haggai challenged and stirred up Zerubbabel the governor, Joshua the high priest and the people, and they resumed the temple project. From August 1, 520 B.C. to August 24th of the same year[3],

---

3   ⁵ibid

the prophet continued to preach to the people until they reverently obeyed God's word. The Lord himself in verse 13 acknowledged the reverence the people showed him. Haggai had succeeded in his first message.

REFLECTION: THE NEED FOR NATIONAL PRIORITY AND COVENANT FAITHFULNESS TO GOD

In this passage of scripture each of the three men played their respective roles in reconstructing their nation (Israel). Haggai's role as a religious personality was delivering every message that God gave to the people.

Zerubbabel as a civil leader also played his part in the reconstruction; he listened to the prophet and mobilized his people to work for their God. Joshua as a priest of the temple made sure the temple worship was correctly restored. With these men at the forefront, the people had no alternative but to work for God. They could have chosen not to but the role model of godly men leading the way with the leading of the Holy Spirit motivated the people to follow God.

THE RELIGIOUS LEADERS

Liberian church leaders should follow the examples of these three men. Like Haggai, They should watch the people they lead; listen to God, rise up and speak for God. The responsibility of pastors of this nation is to tell the people what is pleasing in the sight of God. We must rebuke, correct them whenever they are doing the wrong things. They must always remind them that it is of lack of covenant faithfulness that brought the civil war. The pastors must continue to tell members of their congregations that national prosperity and security, both individually and nationally, depends on covenant faithfulness, yea obedience to God's word (1 King 2:1-4, 3:14). The civil crisis did not only destroy the physical infrastructure of Liberia, but the social, spiritual, and moral standard were destroyed. Persons, who were active members in the churches, had love for God but now have allowed God's work to grow cold in their lives. They have no room for God in their lives and so the temple of God, which is the seat of the Holy Spirit, is now in ruin. The people are only focusing on building fine houses, finding good jobs etc., for themselves while there is no place for God in their lives. Like Haggai, the church leaders, must challenge the people that before they can carry on any reconstruction, they must first rebuild their spiritual lives and have a place for God in their lives.

THE POLITICIANS

The civil leaders should take the lead in presenting themselves to God like Zerubbabel and Joshua who along with the remnant responded wholeheartedly to God's message through the prophet Haggai (Haggai 1:12). It is not always right to say the politicians are responsible for all the troubles in this country. Yes, I agree that for politicians to succeed people have to follow—they may be responsible for a large part but not all of it. Most politicians only seem to be concerned about their families. They use the people to put them in power and when they have the power, they make the people their slaves. They ride in the beautiful cars and live in beautiful houses while the people live in poverty. That's Liberian politics. It is based on selfish ambition, pride, hatred and self-centeredness. They further denigrate their positions by fleeing the countries when problems occur that were of their making, behaving as if they are innocent. This kind of behavior on the part of the politicians must be discouraged. A godly politician will always love his or her country and people and advocate for social reforms that will benefit all.

The people must be first. When you say, "Above all else the people!" you should be sincere, not the opposite. What you promise during election campaigns, must be done when you are elected to office. If there are some conditions that hinder you from fulfilling your promises, please go back to the people and tell them. This will show that you are a person of integrity. When it comes to the characters of a leader, integrity comes first. One of the problems that should be dealt with in nation building is tribal strife. To successfully rebuild the political institution of our country, the politicians also should deal with the tribal strife they have created. Our Politicians thought doing politics on tribal lines could unite the country and that they could easily use the strongest tribal group to put them in power. Sometimes, they succeeded, but look at what happened in the country. We were at tribal war, not civil war! Why were we fighting? Is it for national unity or for tribal dominance in the political arena? Our politicians should rise up and quickly correct this kind of behavior so that it will not be a lasting problem in the rebuilding of our nation.

EVERY LIBERIAN

Every Liberian has a story to tell about the civil war. Whether you lived in Liberia or out of Liberia during the war, the war affected us negatively. One thing that almost all of us did was to pray to God for peace. We made vows to God that once he granted us peace we would serve him faithfully. The Israelites cried for the period of 70 years just to see Zion their motherland but when they returned, they never prioritized God. Similarly, we cried to God for 14 years, but since war ended and some of us returned home, we have forsaken the Lord who granted us peace. We are now involved in dishonesty, secret societies, ritualistic killing and all sorts of worldly activities, which are abominations to God. We do not prioritize God in this nation. We claimed to be a Christian nation but we are not living in accordance with the Christian principles laid down by our founding fathers and mothers.[4]

They signed the covenant with God that they would forever remain faithful and acknowledged the fact that Liberia, "A Home of Glorious Liberty came by God's command."[5] There is nothing mentioned in the Declaration of Independence about a fetish priest (Zoe), Imam or any person from different religious background among signatories. They were all Christians and believed that it was God who had given them the land of Liberia.

If Liberians do not prioritize God, economic hardship and insecurity will still be in our country. We may have well-paid jobs but how we spend our funds is questionable. We do not have peace. We wear fine clothes but we are not satisfied or happy. We must first of all know that our bodies are God's temples; we must glorify God with our bodies (1 Corinthians 6:12-20). Let us be like the people of Haggai's day and quickly arise and rebuild our spiritual houses. Once we prioritize God in our lives, surely we

---

[4]   The Historical Lights of Liberia's Yesterday and Today, P. 279.

[5]   ibid, p. 284-2885.

will have growing interest in Bible study, prayer meeting, outreach, and we will practice honesty, accountability and the spirit of reconciliation.

To reiterate, civil leaders and Liberian citizens should always uphold the fact that this nation belongs to God, and as such they are just stewards accountable to God. But in spite of all the mistakes we have made and the challenge of rebuilding and reconciliation, there is still hope for the future. In the next chapter, you will see how Israel in the midst of her despair, God sent the prophet Haggai to give them hope.

CHAPTER THREE

The Second Oracle:
The Call To Gather Hope And Strength

READING THE SCRIPTURE (HAGGAI 2:1-9)

1. *On the twenty-first of the seventh month, the word of the Lord came by Haggai the prophet saying,*

2. *"Speak now to Zerubbabel the son of Shealtiel, governor of Judah, and to Joshua the son of Jehozadak, the high priest, and the remnant of the people saying,*

3. *Who is left among you who saw this temple in its former glory? And how do you see it now? Does it not seem to you like nothing in comparison?*

4. *But now take courage, Zerubbabel declares the Lord, take courage also Joshua son of Jehozadak the high priest and all you all people of the land take courage, declares the Lord, and work for I am with you, says the Lord of hosts.*

5. *As for the promise, which I made you when you came out of Egypt, My spirit is abiding in your midst, do not fear!*

6. *"For thus says the Lord of hosts, once more in a little while I am going to shake the heavens and the earth, the sea also and the dry land.*

7. *And I will shake all the nations, and they will come with the wealth of all nations, and will fill this house with glory, says the Lord of hosts.*

8. *"The silver is mine, and the gold is mine, declares the Lord of hosts.*

9. *"The latter glory of this house will be greater than the former, says the Lord of host, and in this place I shall hive peace, declares the Lord of Hosts."*

UNDERSTANDING THE SCRIPTURE

Haggai 2:1-3. Although the people started the temple project, there were mixed feelings. Younger priests and Levites from the age of twenty and above were appointed to oversee the work of building the temple. When the foundation was laid they began to praise and thank the Lord for his goodness and loving kindness towards them forever. Yet the elders who had seen the first temple wept because the beauty of the temple did not compare to the splendor of Solomon's temple. As such, they did not feel that the glory of God would be in it again. Notwithstanding, the youth rejoiced because it was their first time to see the temple of God which they had heard about in exile. Because of these different reactions, one could not distinguish the sound of weeping and the shouts of joy (Ezra 3:8-13).

In the midst of this despair, the Lord again sent the prophet Haggai on September 21,520 B.C to encourage the people to be strong and very courageous in rebuilding the temple.[6]

The Lord assured the leaders and the people that:

---

6   Manuel Adjei's Lecture Notes on Biblical Prophets, Ghana Christian College, 1996.

1.   He was going to be with them in as much as they were willing to continue the temple project (Haggai 2:4).

2.   His spirit, as promised to their forefathers when they came out of Egypt, would forever abide with them (Haggai 2:5, Exodus 19:4-6, 29:45, 46).

3.   He would shake the heavens and the earth to pour down his blessings, causing all the nations of the earth to bring to his house what he had blessed them with, for he has control over the wealth of all men (Haggai 2:6, 7,8).

4.   He would fill the present temple with his glory, as such the glory of the present temple would be greater than the former and his peace would be in this temple (Haggai 2:7b-9).

With these assurances from the Lord, the people resumed the rebuilding of the temple[7].

Reflection: LIBERIANS CAN BECOME A BETTER PEOPLE

There are two ways in which we can apply the message of the second oracle to Liberians and their relationship to God. The first is to reflect on how the older generation responded to the rebuilding of the temple. Like the older adults of Haggai's day, the Liberians who lived for decades before the civil war, that is, during the administration of Presidents Tubman and Tolbert, say Liberia's economy is declining and as such life will be the present generation. When an older generation becomes naysayers about the present political and economic state of the nation, they promote little or no hope. This becomes a spiritual problem because God's word calls us to find hope through him. Psalms 9:18 states, "But the needy will not always be forgotten, nor the hope of the afflicted ever perish."

Secondly, we need to reflect on how God can change each one of our lives. The civil war degraded the lives of many devoted Christians. Our bodies which are the temples of God, a dwelling place of the Holy Spirit, were

---

[7]   The Interpreter's One Volume Commentary, P. 502, ed., 1971.

either broken directly or indirectly. Directly in that some of us took an active part in the war. We put Christianity aside and became instruments of destruction. There are unconfirmed reports that some Christians denied the Lordship of Christ just to please man. Sadly, some murdered people, became drunkards, smokers, and prostitutes and were involved in all sorts of wickedness.

Others were broken indirectly in that some of us were forced to be part of something against our will. This is personal testimony which I would like to share. For six months, I was in hiding with my pastor and his family when the fighters of the National Patriot Front of Liberia (NPFL) discovered us in the deep forest of Zahn-Behmon, Nimba County. The fighters forced us to become security guards for the town of Zahn-Behmon. Another time they coerced us to be initiated as a sign of our identity and loyalty to one of the rebel groups. On one occasion I was forced at gunpoint to swim in gravels by the command of one of the fighters, whose name I cannot remember. The rebels had some Christian ladies abused in the presence of their families or relatives. Life became hopeless.

Christians who have had these negative experiences continue to wonder whether the trauma will ever be healed and their spiritual zeal restored. Some believe that God will not forgive them because of the way in which they maltreated people during the crisis. Others have backslidden and continue to live in sin. A friend of ours, who was very active in our youth organization, is now a top security officer. He said that he cannot return to living a Christian life because of his actions during the war. In spite of these beliefs, God is saying:

> Come now, let us reason together," says the Lord,
> "Though your sins are as scarlet, they will be as white
> As snow, though they are red like crimson they will
> Be like wool . . . . (Isaiah 1:18).

Beloved in the Lord let us forget about the past and press forward with faith hoping for the best. Remember, we cannot do anything to change the situation. The scars of the past will always be in our minds and on our bodies, but the grace of God will take us through. Let us lay our burdens at the feet of Jesus for he will give us rest, and then let us sing with the hymn writer Elisa A. Hoffman:

> "I must tell Jesus!
> I cannot bear my burdens alone,
> I must tell Jesus!
> Jesus can help me,
> Jesus alone."[8]

The Apostle Paul is another source of strength and courage. Paul persecuted the church because of his religious zeal, and he was the cause of many Christians dying. Yet Christ redeemed this enemy of God, and Paul became an Apostle who turned the Roman world to Christianity. From Jerusalem to Rome Paul made Christ known.

I read a piece of tract about a man who had murdered a father of a teenage but later became a Christian and started preaching. Under his preaching the boy, whose father he had murdered and who had grown to manhood, accepted Christ and was baptized by the pastor. Lives were transformed. The pastor no longer was seen as a murder in God's eyes, but an instrument of peace. The boy, now a man, had a spirit of forgiveness and reconciliation that could only come through the saving grace of Christ. The Spirit of God was at work within them. What can we learn from this story? Through God's grace we can be changed and our sins washed away. Just as God forgave us our sins, we must forgive others even though they have hurt us.

EXPECTATIONS QUENCHED

In 1997 the election that put former President Charge Taylor into office was held. Truly, all Liberians in the refugee camps and displaced centers were happy when the war was over and a democratically elected government was in control. Expectation was high, with people certain of good governance, improved economic system, free education, good health facilities etc . . . With this hope many Liberians returned home without being repatriated as scheduled by the United Nations High Commission

---

8   Elisha A. Hoffman, Soul-Stirring Songs and Hymns, #371.

for Refugees (UNHCR). But this hope was soon quenched. Older Liberians lamented about the good old days as compared to what they see now, "Liberia will not be a 'Sweet Land of Liberty'. Instead it is 'Bitter Land of slavery'." The younger generation has hope for a better Liberia, but the prevailing circumstance in the country continues to confirm the viewpoint of the older generations.

WHO CAN MAKE THE DIFFERENCE?

In the midst of chaos, where those in leadership cannot change the situation, where there is no constructive contributions from within and without, where no one can be trusted any longer, only the church which Christ Jesus is the head, can make the difference. Like the prophet Haggai, the Bishops, Pastors, Evangelists and lay people of the church in Liberia) are the prophets of the nation. In order to make the difference they must become instruments of peace who bring hope to our leaders and people of this nation. They should pray like St. Francis of Assisi.

> "Lord, make me an instrument of thy peace,
> Where there is hatred, let me show love,
> Where there is injury, pardon,
> Where there is doubt, faith,
> Where there is despair, hope,
> Where there is darkness, light, and
> Where there is sadness, joy . . . ."[9]

Just as Haggai told the Israelites, they should tell the leaders and people of our nation that:

1. God is still on the throne and as such there is hope for the future in spite of the present state of our country and that they should continue the reconstruction of the nation.

2. This 'Glorious Land of Liberty' shall long be ours." They should refute all negative sayings and comments about Liberia and instead

---

9   The Prayer of St. Francis of Assisi, adapted from the Walk To Emmaus Prayer Book, P.5, Copyright Upper Room, 1996.

encourage both old and young that "Liberia will rise again,"[12] with the latter glory of Liberia greater than the former.

3. Liberians (Leaders and people) should prioritize God in every aspect of their individual and national decision-making. The reason why we continue to face serious economic hardship and the sword of war in the land is because we have put God out of our lives and plans. Although we have the form of godliness, we lack the power and zeal of God. The psalmist in psalm 127 says:

"Unless the Lord builds the house
Its builder labor in vain
Unless the Lord watches our the city
The watchmen stand guard in vain."

We must give God place in our nation!

COVENANT FAITHFULNESS NEEDED

The major theme that runs through the entire Old Testament is that covenant faithfulness brings prosperity and security both individually and nationally. When we prioritize God in this nation and live in accordance with the covenant our founding fathers and mothers made with God, we will experience and enjoy the presence of God and economic prosperity.

The presence of God means protection, peace, freedom, love and favor. Like the psalmist in Psalm 127 says, unless God is in the rebuilding process of our nation, our effort will be in vain, unless God himself be the chief security of our nation, our security is in vain. Even though we may be threatened on all sides of our borders and within, we will fear no evil because the Lord is in our midst. Covenant faithfulness call for commitment on the part of all Liberians to God. The leaders and people of this nation should stop practicing the sin of idolatry or allegiance to the gods, which includes "Poro", "Sande", "Freemason", "United-Brother—Friend (UBF)", and all secret societies which undermine our loyalty to the Living God. Boasting of being a Christian nation cannot take anyone to heaven. We should not consult occult medium such as juju or other sources of false protection. We should not make alliance with pagan nations for protection or economic empowerment or else, they will indulge us into ungodly practices such as "same sex marriage." Let us depend fully and solely on God alone, who knows our needs and wants. God will never fail His children who call on him.

God is the source of economic empowerment. God through the prophet Haggai told the people of Israel that "In a little while I will shake the heavens, and the earth, the sea and the dry land and shake all nations and they will bring their wealth and Fill this house." (Haggai 2:6, 7)

The leaders of the church in Liberia should tell our people and leaders that all things belong to God. He controls the natural resources of the earth. He knows where the best mineral deposits are located. He can expose them to our zoologists, geologists, and energy personnel so that Liberia can become a prosperous country. Because God controls the wealth of all nations, including the world's richest nations, He is able to cause those nations to invest in Liberia, bring companies, build factories etc . . . God can bless our economy so that even junior high school children will find vacation jobs and high school graduates will find jobs to save money for a college education. The unemployed from all backgrounds will have opportunities to be employed. Parents will be able to send their children to school. Our public facilities will be revitalized. Just as the Israelites were blessed when they followed God, we too as a nation can be blessed when we follow our Creator and practice covenant faithfulness.

Liberians who live aboard also have a role in rebuilding Liberia, just as the Ghanaians and Nigerians who live abroad. These West African brothers and sisters continue to play vital role in the development of their nations. Some of them do odd jobs, yet they do not forget about their countries. You too can invest in Liberia. Instead of expending energy by saying negative things about your country, determine ways that you can contribute to rebuilding the nation of your birth. You have only one home Liberia, whether you change your location or color or language, you are Liberians. God wrote that in His book that records all people groups.

In July of 2003, when the last peace talk on Liberia was in progress in Accra, the Rev. Dr. John G. Innis, Residence Bishop of the Liberia Annual Conference United Methodist Church, delivered a powerful sermon at the Buduburam United Methodist Church. The service was blessed with the presence of some Liberian clergymen, refugees, and politicians who were attending the Accra Peace Talk. The Bishop was very much uncompromising in his deliberation. I was filled with pity for my country and people, when the Bishop shared his experience from his visit to Gbokongele, a remote village in River Cess County, Liberia.

> "I walked for about eight hours by foot because there is no
> road linking to the village. What I saw in the town was a
> fallen school building . . . . the school kids were writing on
> the ground . . . ."
> The Bishop explained.

Oh what a pity for our country! Could this be our country? After all we have had one hundred and sixty-six plus years of independence. What have we achieved? What have we done for our country?

It is about time for both Liberians at home and abroad to rise up from our selfishness, pride, slumber, hatred and prejudices and make a difference for our nation. Liberians abroad, it was through our country that we got our passports, visa and permit to travel to other lands. We should not be so ungrateful to our motherland. The Lord brought you and I abroad to develop our minds, obtain skills and higher education so that we can be of help to our brothers and sisters including the children of Liberia!

Let me again reiterate that we should imitate our fellow West Africans who even though they live in developed countries, they work tirelessly at developing their country of origin. Like the patriot Nehemiah who worked in the Persian King's palace and when he heard that his country was desolate, he fasted, prayed and gathered resources, returned home and rebuilt the Walls of Jerusalem. I know that one of the excuses we can give is that the country is not yet safe. Remember, Nehemiah never had it easy. There were strong oppositions, but with the Lord on his side, he prevailed. Come home let us rebuild a better nation in which we can develop right relationship with one another irrespective of our ethnic backgrounds. There is a familiar song that says,

> "The more we are together

the happier we shall be.
Mine friend is yours friends.
Yours friend is my friend."

Living together is necessary because there is strength in being together and this can make us a strong people and nation.

CHAPTER FOUR

The Third Oracle:
The Call To Right Relationship
With Our Fellow Men

READING THE SCRIPTURE (HAGGAI 2:10-19)

10. *On the twenty-fourth of the ninth month, in the second year of Darius, the word of the Lord came to Haggai the prophet saying,*

11. *"Thus says the Lord of host, Ask now the priest for ruling:*

12. *If a man carries holy meat in the fold of his garment, and torches bread with this fold, or cooked food, wine, oil, or any other food, will it become holy? "And the priests answered and said no."*

13. *Then Haggai said, "If one who is unclean from a corpse touches any of these, will the latter become unclean?*

14. *Then Haggai answered and said, "So is this people. And so is this nation before me," declares the Lord, "and so is every work of their hands" and so is every work of their hands, and what they offer there is unclean.*

15. *"But now, do consider from this day onward before one stone was paced on another in the temple of the Lord,*

16. *From that time when one came to a grain heap of twenty measures, there would be only ten, and when one came to the wine vat to draw fifty measures, there would be only twenty.*

17. *"I smote you and every work of your hands with blasting wind, mildew, and hail, yet you did not come back to me declares the Lord.*

18. *"Do consider from this day onward, from the twenty-fourth day of the ninth month, from the day when the temple of the Lord was founded, consider:*

19. *"Is there seed still in the barn? Even including the vine, the fig tree, the pomegranate, and the olive tree, it has not borne fruit. Yet from this day on I will bless you."*

UNDER STANDING THE SCRIPTURE

Haggai 2:10-19. The third oracle came on December 18, 520 BC[10] during the second year of Darius' rule; it was winter season when crops were planted. The prophet used an analogy to teach the effect of righteousness and unrighteousness as well as national and individual responsibility. The prophet called on the priests to witness that, it is the unclean, rather than the clean, which is contagious. The prophet used this analogy to make the following important points.

1. Holiness is not contagious, nor is it easily transmitted, but it is an individual responsibility. God holds every one responsible for his or her sin. Haggai 2:10-13

2. Evil is contagious for it spreads very fast and it influences people more than holiness. Even though the Israelites were back in the temple worshiping they were disobedient to God and still living in sin. The priests who were consecrated to serve the Lord

---

10   Manuel Adjei

defiled themselves with the people as they interacted. The priests' response to the question Haggai asked in verses 12 and 13 of chapter two is in line with Leviticus 26 and Numbers 19:11-13, 22. Leviticus 25 speaks of transmitting holiness, when a person touches a consecrated sacrifice; he or she becomes holy because it is a direct contact. But the garment cannot pass that holiness to a third object. Number 19 addresses ceremonial uncleanness, which is easily transmitted because once a person touches a corpse he or she becomes unclean. This is how the Lord described the people and nation of Israel who were living unclean lives. Whatever they did was defiled before God.

3. Careful thought should be given to their deeds as they rebuilt the temple. The Lord reminded them that they had not given to his work generously. As such, economic prosperity was withheld from the Israelites and instead they experienced blight, mildew, and, hail as a reward for their disobedience (Haggai 2:15-19a).

4. Even their possessions belong to the Lord and should be used to help continue building the temple. Here the Lord was saying that covenant faithfulness brings prosperity and security. Considering the peoples' effort in rebuilding the temple, the Lord promised them divine blessing provided they practice holiness and give generously to his work (Haggai 2:19b).

REFLECTION: The Effects of the Civil War on Liberians

The civil crisis almost caused every Liberian to take God serious and depended on him for survival in the midst of all the suffering, and hopelessness. Many Liberians in displaced centers and refugee camps became Christians. Even the people on the "Bulk Challenge," the battered freighter that carried over 3,0000 desperate Liberians refugees to Ghana, attended prayer meetings and devotion. In desperation, as Liberians, we acknowledged that true peace and safety can only be found in the arms of God, so we humbly turned to God for help.

Few instances that showed Liberians commitment to the Lord was during the war. All the main line churches and independent churches at the displaced and refugee camps were represented by their congregations. I can remember very well when we fled to the Ivory Coast in 1990, we had one congregation comprising of all the denominations in Liberia. When we settled down and began to identify one another, the need arose for us to group under the Leadership of our individual denomination. This went on everywhere even at the Buduburam Refugee camp in Ghana.

These churches were packed every Sunday and people were involved in Christian related activities in all refugee camps and displaced centers. Since Liberia has returned to peace many Christians have grown cold in their commitment. Their Christianity was only for exile life. Nowadays, the same people who called out to God in exile do not have time for family devotion, Bible study and prayer meetings. They only go to church on Sunday to show their suits or to meet their friends or because of tradition. Sunday has become a day of relaxation on the beaches or at amusement centers for many Liberian Christians, not a day of worshiping God.

As Liberians, let us search out and examine our ways as to whether we are really a Christian nation. Liberians are involved with all sorts of wicked deeds and immoral acts. It is very surprising to note that some of the brothers and sisters who receive communion in the churches are involve in ritualistic killing and secret societies. They sit under the preaching and hear the divine word of God, yet they hurt and kill innocent people. The scripture describes this double standard in Titus 1:16 that they profess to know God but in deeds they deny him. They have the outward form of godliness but they lack the power of God.

Another alarming development is that Liberian adults and children are indulging in all form of sexual immoralities. A friend of mine, Peter S. Dolo, in his Gospel Album, "See the Grace" said, "Bestiality, Homosexuality, Lesbianism, Fornication, Adultery etc., are the talk of the day . . . ."[11] People do not take the warning in Galatians 5:19-21 that a person, who indulgences himself or herself in the foregoing, will not inherit God's Kingdom.

---

[11] Peter S. Dolo in his Gospel Album: See The Grace, a Flomo Theatre Production Studio, Gbarnga City, Liberia, 2001.

The situation in our country can be compared to the days of the Judges where everyone did what was right in his own eyes (Judges 21:25). This was the time Israel had departed from covenant faithfulness, a standard of conduct found in the Law. As a result there was insecurity and economic hardship in Israel. As Liberians we should, always remember that covenant faithfulness brings national and individual prosperity and security. Let us not only seek God with all of our heart in time of trouble but also when we are living in peace.

THE ROOT OF ECONOMIC HARDSHIP

As we read throughout the Old Testament, we see the continual pattern of the Israelites facing economic hardship because they did not follow or give their work to God. Why should God treat us any differently? Like the people of Haggai's day, God has withheld his blessing from Liberians because we have turned our back on him. When we turn our back on God, we end up following our own selfish desires, which inevitably leads to poor decisions and only focusing on self-fulfillment. This type of selfish individualism leads to the decay and corruption of society. In contrast, when we obediently respond to the grace of God with our gift, time, life, services, our attitudes change and our spirits become open to God's leading and blessings (Haggai 2: 18, 19).

Where you see Christianity flourishing, you see Christians generously giving to God's work whether it is time, money or both. The work of God becomes their main priority and they have the most valuable type of prosperity, a sense of peace and fulfillment that can only come from God. Remember that God can only use us when we set ourselves aside for his glory and purpose of pleasing him. We should seriously search out, examine our ways and turn back to the Lord and he will heal our land.

CHAPTER FIVE

The Fourth Oracle: The Assurance Of God's Vengeance On Wicked Leaders And Nations That Shed Liberians Blood

READING THE SCRIPTURE HAGGAI (2:20-23)

20. *The word of the Lord came the second time to Haggai on the twenty-fourth day of the month saying,*

21. *"Speak to Zerubbabel governor of Judah saying, "I am going to shake the heaven and the earth.*

22. *"And I will overthrow the thrones of kingdoms and destroy the power of the kingdoms of the nations, and I will overthrow chariot and their riders will go by sword of another.*

23. *"On that day" declares the Lord of host, I will take you, Zerubbabel, sons of Sheathiel, my servants, declares the Lord, "and I will make you like a signet ring, for I have chosen you declares the Lord of Host."*

UNDERSTANDING THE SCRIPTURE: PROMISE OF BLESSING & VEGEANCE

In this oracle (**Haggai 2:20-23**), the Lord made another promise, he would cause rich countries to invest in Israel in order to rescue her (2:7). The prophet was instructed by the Lord to inform the Governor, Zerubbabel, that besides causing rich countries to be of blessing to the nation of Israel; God was going to overthrow world powers, which had rebelled against him and had mistreated his chosen people (2:21-22). This was a powerful prophecy by Haggai; the Israelites would have immediately related back to their oral history of how God had overthrown powerful kingdoms and nations of Egypt, Assyria and Babylonia.[12]

Background Study of Kingdoms That Oppressed Israel [13]

Egypt—Egypt was the first cradle of civilization. She existed as a world's power of the Mediterranean from about 2100 BC up to 1220 BC. At this time in the history, Egypt supplied the whole world during the great famine. The Bible reported that people came from the Middle East to buy food in Egypt. (Gen. 42:1ff)

During the second intermediate period, Hyksos dynasty began to control (1800-1600 BC) Egypt. During the first half of the 19th Dynasty, the oppression of God's people (Israel) by Hyksos kings began, and was later followed by the Exodus (16-1100 BC). This mistreatment of God's people led to God's 10 plagues and the subsequent death of every first male born of Egypt (Exodus 7-11).

When Israel settled in the Promised Land and established the monarchy, under the able leadership of King David and his son Solomon, Israel became one of the most powerful and prosperous nations in the Mediterranean world. Her enemies were defeated; she was in control of all the land promised to Abraham (Genesis 15:18). Her borders extended from Egypt to the Euphrates, in the Persian Gulf. During this Golden Age of Israel, Egypt was no longer a world power and so under the rule of

---

12   The Lion's Handbook to the Bible, pp. 660-661.

13   ibid

King Solomon there was a marriage alliance between Israel and Egypt for a political reason. Even though God had warned Israel about marriage to foreigners (Numbers 25:1-15), Solomon married the daughter of Pharaoh. This later led Solomon to apostasy.

Assyria—When Assyria threatened Israel's southern kingdom (Judah), she sought protection from Egypt. God warned Judah's King Hezekiah concerning this alliance telling him that He had raised Assyria as the world power to destroy Egypt. This was because Egypt has been a destroyer of God's people (Isaiah 33; 1). In 701 BC Sennacherib of Assyria attacked Judah, and Egypt's King Pharaoh Shebitku sent his brother, Tirhakah, to help Judah but was defeated twice. True to God's prophecy, the Assyrians conquered both Judah and Egypt.

The Assyrian Rule—the next powerful nation that God destroyed before the time of Haggai's prophecy was Assyria. During the second millennium BC, Assyria dominated the Mediterranean world (135 BC-612 BC). God used Assyria as an agent of judgment for Israel. Scriptures affirm that God establishes government of nations for His glory not for man's glory. There is no authority except that which God has ordained (Romans 13).

In 722 B.C the Assyrians captured Northern Palestine and deported all its citizens, leaving only the disabled people in the land. Assyrian was very cruel in treating her captives. It is reported in history, (even the Old Testament book of Nahum) that leaders and people of conquered nations were tortured, with their blood flowing like a stream down the side of the mountain before their executioners. Because of this cruelty God, through the prophet Jonah, announced the destruction of Assyria, but they repented and God subsequently forgave them (see the book of Jonah). Not long after, the Assyrians reverted to their extremes weakness, brutality and pride. This wickedness reached its peak under Ashurbanipal. (669 B.C). The prophet Nahum predicted the fall of Assyria as God's judgment upon her for mistreating his people (Nahum 1-3).

The Neo-Babylonian Rule—Another world power that God raised to discipline wicked kingdoms was Babylonia. This new world power in the Mediterranean reigned from 612 B.C to 539 B.C under the able leadership of Nebuchadnezzar. Again when Judah forsook the Lord, and sought other gods for protection, God warned them through the prophet Jeremiah that he would use Nebuchadnezzar to besiege Judah (Jeremiah 25:1-11). In 538 B.C. Nebuchadnezzar besieged Jerusalem and took all its inhabitants away (2 Kings 24:1-7; Daniel 1:1-7) burning the city of Jerusalem.

Nebuchadnezzar became proud and began to boast about his might, power and glory. God removed him from his throne and Nebuchadnezzar spend seven years in the bush as a deranged man. (Daniel 4:28-34ff). The Lord had predicted this event through the prophet Jeremiah before the captured of Jerusalem in 538 B.C. (Jeremiah 23:12-38).

The Mede-Persian Empire—However, God remembered his promise to Israel. At the end of the 70 years in exile God raised up another agent of judgment against Babylon for mistreating his people, Israel. God used Cyrus of Persia, who he referred to as his shepherd; to set the Jews free and rebuild Jerusalem (Isaiah 44:28)

In 539 B.C Babylon fell to the Persians under the leadership of Cyrus. In accordance with God's word, Cyrus and his allies repaid the Babylonians for their cruelty and wickedness against God's people. Cyrus' edict allowed all Jews to return home, rebuild Jerusalem, and put in place the religious and political system (Ezra 1:1-4)

In actuality, the prophecy of Haggai as contained in chapter 2:20-23, came to fulfillment when the Jews returned home in 538 B.C. Ultimately this prophecy will be fulfilled when Christ comes in his final victory to establish his everlasting throne. There will be destruction of God's enemy and deliverance for God's people.

REFLECTION: THE JUDGEMENT OF GOD—HIS VENGEANCE ON LIBERIANS WHO MALTREATED THEIR FELLOW LIBERIANS

The fourth oracle of Haggai's relevancy to our situation as Liberians is twofold. First of all, we shall consider how our fellow brothers and sisters who had arms treated their fellow Liberians during the 14 years old war. Secondly we shall look at the role of foreign powers.

berians, especially the
om. When an NPFL
they had come to free
overnment almost all
imba were skeptical,
r nightmare like that
ion of properties. As
nd killing citizens of
y to pledge support
justifiable reason.

During the first six
innocent people's
or oppressors; the
nd liberty. Many
along the major
being members of
the 1985 election
heir working I.D.
f their husbands

tion Movement
he ULIMO –K
se Force (LDF),
PFL), Liberians
h split into the
nitted the same

the Liberian
dehumanize
hat they had
were wolves
nd primitive
and Liberia's
ntributed a

unched an attack
ecember 1989, its
y corrupt and full
s such, the NPFL
iberia and establish
)oe government had
ic groups, which he
eat to his leadership.
ernment to eliminate
those ethnic groups.
vonkpah's coupe d'état
uawonkpah and people
and murdered by Doe's
Terrorist Unit). This was

Nimbanians were accused
s who hailed from Nimba
. They were arrested in the
en to unknown destinations.

nta United Methodist School;
mily in Geneyeelu, a suburb of
re we stayed was picked up by
killed. Fear gripped us and we
on for safety but that was not safe
We had to hide our identities in
Ganta to Gbranga and into Yela
nto Nimba County, by way of the
r's hometown, Zahn Behmon and
t for six months. During that time
safe drinking water and other basic
itional forms of producing salt and
and roosters were killed with the fear
vernment soldiers or the rebels would
us. But we were later captured by the
this, God was with us.

31

IN THE MIDST OF THESE ATROCITIES, L
oppressed, cried out yearning for relief and freed
spokesman announced on international media that
the Liberia people from oppression of the Doe led
Liberians believed them. However the people of N
because they did not want to be caught up in anothe
of 1985 that caused the death of citizens and destruc
mentioned above, when Government began hunting
Nimba County, it caused the people of Nimba Coun
to the NPFL in self-defense, even though it was an u

Unfortunately, NPFL repeated the same atrocities.
months of NPFL presence on the soil of Liberia, man
blood was shed. The liberators became the captors
freedom fighters became the destroyers of freedom
people were slaughtered in cold blood at checkpoint
roads and highways of Liberia. People were killed for
certain tribal groups. Some were killed for possession of
voter's registration I.D. card, while others for possessing t
cards. Worst of all, women were raped in the presence
and family members.

Other warring factions were just as bad. The United Liber
for Democracy in Liberia (ULIMO), which later becan
and ULIMO-J, Liberia Peace Council (LPC), Lofa Defen
the Independent National Patriotic Front of Liberia (IN
United for Reconciliation and Democracy (LURD), whic
Movement for Democracy in Liberia (MODEL), all comm
atrocities against the people of Liberia.

Usually these groups claimed that they had come to save
people, but they sang the same song and used the same tools t
the people. Even though many of these groups claimed t
broken away from the NPFL because of their atrocities, the
in sheep's clothing. Because of the carnage, heartlessness a
behavior of these warring factions, schools, hospitals, clinics
infrastructure was destroyed. These groups still have not c
cent to the reconstruction of our country.

When The National Patriotic Front of Liberia (NPFL) launched an attack on the government of President Samuel K. Doe in December 1989, its official reasons was that the Doe government was very corrupt and full of injustices, dishonesty, tribalism and nepotism. As such, the NPFL claimed that they had come to liberate the people of Liberia and establish a government of inclusion and national unity. The Doe government had committed unwholesome acts against certain ethnic groups, which he felt, had undermined his government and was a threat to his leadership. Many false coupe d'états were organized by the government to eliminate senior officials of his government who were from those ethnic groups. In November 1985, when General Thomas Quawonkpah's coupe d'état failed and Doe survived, those who supported Quawonkpah and people from his tribe and region, were hunted, tortured and murdered by Doe's death squad known as the SATU (Special Anti-Terrorist Unit). This was done without investigation or trail.

Similar brutal acts were repeated in 1989 when Nimbanians were accused of being the top fighters in the NPFL. Persons who hailed from Nimba County were hunted in every parts of Liberia. They were arrested in the night by gunmen and at checkpoints and taken to unknown destinations. Their families were unable to see them.

During this time, I was a student at the Ganta United Methodist School; living with Reverend Jacob Nyaquoi and family in Geneyeelu, a suburb of Ganta. An officer who lived closed to where we stayed was picked up by government security in the night and was killed. Fear gripped us and we fled to the Ganta United Methodist Mission for safety but that was not safe either. We left for the pastor's hometown. We had to hide our identities in order to cross security checkpoints from Ganta to Gbranga and into Yela Mission in Bong County. We crossed into Nimba County, by way of the St. John River. We traveled to the pastor's hometown, Zahn Behmon and ended up in the Neegeleah Rain Forest for six months. During that time we had no table salt, medication, soap, safe drinking water and other basic human needs. We turned to the traditional forms of producing salt and soap items in order to survive. Dogs and roosters were killed with the fear that when they barked or crowed government soldiers or the rebels would discover our hiding place and hunt us. But we were later captured by the rebels but were unharmed. In all of this, God was with us.

31

IN THE MIDST OF THESE ATROCITIES, Liberians, especially the oppressed, cried out yearning for relief and freedom. When an NPFL spokesman announced on international media that they had come to free the Liberia people from oppression of the Doe led government almost all Liberians believed them. However the people of Nimba were skeptical, because they did not want to be caught up in another nightmare like that of 1985 that caused the death of citizens and destruction of properties. As mentioned above, when Government began hunting and killing citizens of Nimba County, it caused the people of Nimba County to pledge support to the NPFL in self-defense, even though it was an unjustifiable reason.

Unfortunately, NPFL repeated the same atrocities. During the first six months of NPFL presence on the soil of Liberia, many innocent people's blood was shed. The liberators became the captors or oppressors; the freedom fighters became the destroyers of freedom and liberty. Many people were slaughtered in cold blood at checkpoints along the major roads and highways of Liberia. People were killed for being members of certain tribal groups. Some were killed for possession of the 1985 election voter's registration I.D. card, while others for possessing their working I.D. cards. Worst of all, women were raped in the presence of their husbands and family members.

Other warring factions were just as bad. The United Liberation Movement for Democracy in Liberia (ULIMO), which later became ULIMO –K and ULIMO-J, Liberia Peace Council (LPC), Lofa Defense Force (LDF), the Independent National Patriotic Front of Liberia (INPFL), Liberians United for Reconciliation and Democracy (LURD), which split into the Movement for Democracy in Liberia (MODEL), all committed the same atrocities against the people of Liberia.

Usually these groups claimed that they had come to save the Liberian people, but they sang the same song and used the same tools to dehumanize the people. Even though many of these groups claimed that they had broken away from the NPFL because of their atrocities, they were wolves in sheep's clothing. Because of the carnage, heartlessness and primitive behavior of these warring factions, schools, hospitals, clinics and Liberia's infrastructure was destroyed. These groups still have not contributed a cent to the reconstruction of our country.

Humanly speaking Liberians, like the Jews of Haggai's Day, are trying their best to forget about the past and reconcile with their enemies, de-traumatize their minds and rebuild the nation morally and spiritually. Yet as we seek peace and reconciliation important questions are raised. Will Liberia regain her status? Why does God allow war criminals to live freely in our beloved nation and not bring them to justice? Questions abound and ring in our minds?

Sadly, many of the warlords still feel that they had a just cause for committing such grave atrocities against the people of Liberia. Let me serve a warning to those of you who committed these atrocities. Liberia as part of the global village will be involved in rendering judgment against you for what you have done. Babies will serve on the judge's panel and they will tell you I remember when you were killing my mother, my father, my brother, and my sister. What a pity! Ultimately God will judge you for all that you have done against your own people oh warlords, even those deeds that no one saw you committing! You have the chance, and that is now, to tell the people of Liberia that you are sorry and then turn to God in repentance (refer to Appendix A for help). But your end will be sad if you refuse to obey the voice of God.

GOD'S VEAGENCE ON FOREIGN NATIONS WHO SHED LIBERIANS' BLOOD

Some world powers and nations also shared directly or indirectly in destroying life and properties in Liberia. Arms and ammunition exchange occurred for mineral resources in Liberia. Some West African countries such as Ivory Coast, Sierra Leone, Guinea, and Burkina Faso became breeding centers for rebels and foreign aggression against the people of Liberia. Even those peacekeepers (ECOMONG) sent by ECOWAS committed atrocities against Liberia. The series of air bombing carried out by ECOMONG, though intended for rebels' position, hit civilian positions, with life and properties were destroyed. (Need spell out what ECOMONG stands for)

Notwithstanding, there is hope for the people of Liberia. This hope is found in the word of God; who is our comforter, protector, and the author and finisher of our faith. His joy is our strength. Let us forget about the past "and press forward with our eyes fixed on God. We should not have a spirit of revenge based on the past or the present. For the Lord says, "Vengeance is mine I will repay" (Romans 12:19). As God's people, let us love and pray for them for they did not know what they were doing. God has his own way of punishing wicked people. For instance, all the nations that shared in the suffering and desolation of the Israelites were punished by God. Hear what the Bible has to say about God's judgment against Babylon:

> "And Babylon, the glory of kingdoms, the beauty of the Chaldeans' pride, shall be as when God overthrew Sodom and Gomorrah. It shall never be inhabited, neither shall it be dwelt in from generation to generation: neither shall the Arabian pitch tent there; neither shall shepherds make their flocks to lie down there. But wild beasts of the desert shall lie there; and their houses shall be full of doleful creatures; and ostriches shall dwell there, and wild goats shall dance there. And wolves shall cry in their castles, and jackals in the pleasant palaces: and her time is near to come, and her days shall not be prolonged."
>
> (Isaiah 13:19-22)

God's judgment against Assyria:

> "That I will break the Assyrian in my land, and upon my mountains tread him under foot: then shall his yoke depart from off them, and his burden depart from off their shoulder. This is the purpose that is purposed upon the whole earth; and this is the hand that is stretched out upon all the nations. For Jehovah of hosts hath purposed, and who shall annul it? And his hand is stretched out, and who shall turn it back?"
>
> (Isaiah 14:25-27)

There are numerous examples in Old Testament prophecies of God punishing nations who harmed Israel; the most serious examples were Assyria and Babylon. The book of Nahum records the destruction of Assyria (Nahum 1-3). The Persians destroyed the Babylonians. (Jeremiah 50:1-46.)

This is what the Lord says:

> "Thus saith Jehovah: Though they are in full strength, and likewise many, even so shall they be cut down, and he shall pass away. Though I have afflicted thee, I will afflict thee no more. And now will I break his yoke from off thee, and will burst thy bonds in sunder. And Jehovah hath given commandment concerning thee, that no more of thy name be sown: out of the house of thy gods will I cut off the graven image and the molten image; I will make thy grave; for thou art vile. Behold, upon the mountains the feet of him that bringeth good tidings that preached peace! Keep thy feasts, O Judah, perform thy vows; for the wicked one shall no more pass through thee; he is utterly cut off" (Nahum 1:12-3:11).

> "Declare you among the nations and publish, and set up a standard; publish, and conceal not: say, Babylon is taken, Bel is put to shame, Merodach is dismayed; her images are put to shame, her idols are dismayed. For, lo, I will stir up and cause to come up against Babylon a company of great nations from the North Country; and they shall set themselves in array against her; from thence she shall be taken: their arrows shall be as of an expert mighty man; none shall return in vain" (Jeremiah 50:2, 9).

As the saying goes," when you see your neighbor's house on fire, help to put it out, because the same day it may be yours." As you may have observed, some West African Countries like Sierra Leone, Guinea and the Ivory Coast have troubles because of the way in which they treated Liberians. They saw Liberian in crisis but did not help. ECOMONG's first military base was built on Sierra Leone's soil. Jet bombers picked up from these places and bombed innocent civilians in Liberia. Sierra Leone, Guinea and Ivory Coast are our closet neighbors who used their soils to train rebels—NPFL, MODEL, ULIMO and LURD rebels. Before the war many Africans including Guineans, Sierra Leoneans, and Ivoirians, lived and worked in Liberia for economic and political reasons. Instead of persuading their governments to help rebuild Liberia, they helped to destroy Liberia. As we watch Sierra Leone, Guinea, and Ivory Coast struggle with their own troubles, it raises the question if this is a judgment from God because of the way they treated Liberia.

Credit must be given to Ghanaians and Nigerians as well as the United Nations, which are helping Liberians to get the peace we deserve. God will surely reward you for your good work. Remember: "Happy are those who work for peace, God will call them His Children!" (Matthew 5:9).

The Lord told Haggai that he was going to overthrow kingdoms and destroy their powers. The Lord will humble all the nations that have shared in the destruction of Liberia. I believe strongly that what is happening in the physical realm is also happening in the spiritual realm. The forces of darkness manipulated people and used them to commit all the atrocities that were carried out against Liberians. When Christ comes in his final victory he will judge the world and establish his perfect kingdom. God's people will be free at last.

All Liberians should come together for the reconciliation and reconstruction of our broken nation. No one can build our nation better than what we can do. Arms and negative propaganda are not tools for rebuilding. Come let us reconcile and rebuild Liberia.

CONCLUSION

Our priority as Liberians at home and abroad should be confession, forgiveness, reconciliation and reconstruction. True reconciliation calls for confession and forgiveness. Realistically, confession on the part of those who hurt their fellow Liberians, and forgiveness on the part of those who were hurt by their fellow Liberians. Remember that God cannot forgive anyone who does not forgive his or her brother or sister. Sometimes the fear of being hunted by those we have hurt hinders us from going to tell them that we are sorry. The Lord will give you the word and the power to do so. Trust Him in the process. In David Wilkerson's book (1962), "The Cross and The Switchblade," Nicky Cruz shared his experience about a long time enemy. Prior to his conversion to Christ, Nicky had been a notorious gang leader in New York and in one of his fights, he beat a rival gang. This rival gang tried many times to retaliate but could not succeed. According to Nicky, he was speaking to a large crowd in one of his mass crusades. To his uttermost surprise, when he made the altar call, this long time enemy who had come purposefully to kill Nicky, went forward for the altar call. When Nicky saw him among the crowd his stomach boiled inside him, thinking that he was finished. His enemy walked up to him and they embraced; when he crossed his hands across his back, he felt a gun under his coat. The man confessed that he had been looking for Nicky and when he heard about the crusade, he came to kill him. When the man heard Nicky preach about how God forgives us through Jesus Christ His Son in spite of our wicked deeds he was convicted. He admitted that the message touched him so much that he changed his mind and could not understand why(especially the statement that "it cost God so much to let His only Son Jesus Christ, to die in our place"). Both men cried with tears and felt relieved. God can help you too.

It is true that no one has the right to unjustly hurt anyone. However, the God of the universe is the only Judge for human action and has given every nation a code of laws that can be used to administer justice. Remember that the crisis did not begin 14 years ago (1989); the seed of the war was sown long before some of us were born. A careful analysis shows that the seed of the war was sown before 1822 and was being nurtured from the founding of Liberia up to our time. But see where it has taken us. It has taken us from our position as the First Black African Republic and the Cradle of Africa's Democracy to a war ravaged, barbaric and troublesome nation. We brought liberty to Africa and we in turn abused liberty!

We can recover and regain our position as the first in Africa, but this can only be possible when reconcile and rebuild our nation for all Liberians, not for a particular tribal or ethnic group.

We want to be grateful to the first post war government for how it has maintained the peace. Liberia is back in its proper position among the community of nations. Our nation has seen some level of economic growth and prosperity, and we continue to enjoy some level of security and freedom of expression. We can support our nation and leadership by being faithful stewards and ambassadors of peace and development.

Liberians, we have learned enough from where we find ourselves, either as refugees or permanent residents or students etc. We have much to give to Liberia. It is time for us to make the right investment to rebuild our nation. What I would like to propose to both Liberians at home and abroad is that we work together to transform the war machineries we used to kill our fellow Liberians into foundations that can help rebuild the moral, social, and economic infrastructures of our nation and its people. Let us come together and write proposals for the rehabilitation of our young people, especially, ex-combatants and orphans. Let us build programs that will accelerate the education of those who have passed normal school age. Let us begin to think positively about our country and the well-being of its people!

Finally, fellow Liberians let us follow the example of the people of Haggai's Day who set right priorities. When they did this God provided security, prosperity and healed their land and they succeeded in the rebuilding of their nation and national heritage. Ultimately God will wipe away our tears, destroy our enemy's, restore our economic prosperity and give us security. Then we will proudly sing: "All Hail! Liberia Hail, this glorious Land of (sweet) liberty shall long be ours"! The Lord has spoken to you and to me. What is your response?

Appendix A

Steps to Peace and Healing

Peace vs. Vengeance

Seigbe was a boarding student at BWI when he learned that government soldiers loyal to President Doe entered his village and killed his parents, brothers and sisters. Immediately a fog of pain and bewilderment surrounded him. He could not stand the grief and could not find any justifiable reason why his people were killed. All that came to his mind was to revenge. When the rebel fighters loyal to Taylor reached Kakata, Seigbe joined them and started fighting alongside the rebels. He even became a General. He was not happy when ECOWAS countries started talking about ceasefire and peace talk. "Peace is not my language," he cried, "I will kill all those who killed my people!" Sadly enough, Seigbe was hit by stray bullet one morning and was killed.

Fellow Liberians, we all are like Seigbe in one way or another. When life is going on well, peace of mind comes easily, but feelings of peace are fragile and what usually comes to mind is revenge. Any problem that comes along can destroy our feelings of peace. When your peace is upset, one common reaction is to run away from the situation or face it with bitterness. Sometimes we tend to break relationships, disown the other person, tribes or make that group our lifetime enemy. Running away will not solve the problem.

People who were once classmates, workmates, and even married were not able to sit down and agree on a peaceful solution one thing that could make the difference in the life of all Liberians.

Like Seigbe, they cried, "Peace is not my language . . ." Meanwhile we must remember what peace does to a nation and its people.

Peace keeps us together as—we need peace that will hold us steady, that will stay right side up when our world is turned upside down. We need a deep inner peace that is not based on changing circumstances or having position in the government.

Peace causes us to turn to God—when we are stunned by the emotional and physical trauma of crisis; we often make a deliberate choice to turn to God or away from him. Through Jesus Christ, God has invited tribes and every people group of Liberia, no matter how hurt or discouraged we are, to call upon Him in our time of trouble for peace that only comes from Him. "My peace I give you. I do not give to you as the world gives." (John 14:27).

Peace helps to focus our minds on God when hurtful feelings overwhelm us—when you seems to picture the past, try to focus your thoughts on the goodness of God and say "The Lord is my light and my salvation—of whom shall I fear? The Lord is the stronghold of my life—of whom shall I be afraid?" Let us make it our priority to be at peace with our fellow Liberians. We should not blame anyone. Great nations of the world had experienced what we just went through.

God Can Heal the Wounds of War

When my wife Martha died, I thought I would die. She was the most important person in my life. My heart was wounded. I cried all night but she could not be found. I did not know where to turn. People came one after another but could not help me. All I could do was to cry out to God. I cried and prayed every night so that God could heal my broken heart. He touched my life and since then I have been a source of healing to other people in need.

The civil crisis has caused every Liberian hurtful pain one way or another. Maybe your loved one was killed or you experienced something like rape, beating, looting of your property, harassments etc. Remember God can heal you and your life can become normal again. In order to be healed you can follow these steps.

Talk to someone

Talk about how you feel, your negative experiences, to someone you trust such as your friend, pastor, a counselor, or any religious person who can help you overcome your problem. When you keep your feelings inside you, it will make you sick, depressed, and you will feel as if life is useless. The apostle Paul admonishes the Christians at Galatia to carry each other burdens so as to fulfill the law of God. (See Gal. 6:2.)

Do not blame yourself

Blaming yourself for what has happened will not help you. Know that this world is not free of evil people. Do not let thoughts play over-and-over in your mind about how you were treated by someone doing the war; just forgive them just as Jesus asked God to forgive those who were killing Him on the cross. (See Luke 23:34). I had a terrible experience during the war when a gentleman with a single barrel compelled me to swim in gravel. I was on the ground while he was pointing his gun at me. I rolled myself in that gravel back and forth until he was satisfied. But one thing that God has done for me is that I cannot even picture who this gentleman is.

Give Yourself Time to Heal

It will take you time to heal; we are healed by the wounds of our Lord Jesus Christ (I Peter 2:24). Know that your physical or emotional wounds will not vanish instantly. I believe if we follow these steps, we will make it right with those who hurt us. Speak out your hurts and begin to call on God right now and it shall be well with you all the days of your life and you will live with your neighbor in peace.

You may use your own words or use the following prayer:

> *Dear Lord Jesus Christ, I need you right now because I am hurt and in need of your healing, peace and grace. I also realize that I have hurt you because as sinner I have not forgiven those who have hurt me. I cannot solve my own problems. I believe that on the cross you solved all of my problems. I turn to you right now from all my revengeful spirit and will now follow you as a peacemaker. I promised that from this day onwards I will love those who have hurt me. Create in me a clean heart and renew a right spirit within me. Thank you for your grace and forgiveness. I now vow to be your follower!*
>
> *I pray in the name of Jesus. Amen!*

APPENDIX B

Familiar Liberian Songs

"The Liberian National Anthem"

I.   All hail, Liberia, hail! (All hail!)
All hail, Liberia, hail! (All hail!)
This glorious land of liberty
Shall long be ours.
Though new her name,
Green be her fame,
And mighty be her powers,
And mighty be her powers.
In joy and gladness,
With our hearts united,
We'll shout the freedom,
Of a race benighted.
Long live Liberia, happy land!
A home of glorious liberty,
By God's command!
A home of glorious liberty,
By God's command!

II. All hail, Liberia, hail! (All hail!)
     All hail, Liberia, hail! (All hail!)
     In union strong success is sure.
     We cannot fail!
     With God above,
     Our rights to prove,
     We will o'er all prevail,
     We will o'er all prevail!
     With heart and hand our country's cause defending,
     We'll meet the foe with valour unpretending.
     Long live Liberia, happy land!
     A home of glorious liberty,
     By God's command!
     A home of glorious liberty,
     By God's command!

The Lyrics of the National Anthem was written by President Daniel Bashiel Warner (1815-1880, 3rd president of Liberia) and music by Olmstead Luca, an African-American, who lived at the time (1826-1869). Adapted and became the official national anthem in 1847.

"LIBERIA"

Liberia! Sweet land of liberty,
We prophesize to you, you will rise
You will shine,
You will proper in Africa,
Yea the world! (2x)

Liberia you are lifted, Amen!
Hallelujah, Amen
Liberia you are lifted Amen
Hallelujah

We prophesize to you
You will proper Amen!
Hallelujah, Amen!
Liberia you are lifted Amen!

"JESUS LOVES ALL LIBERIANS

1. Jesus loves all Liberians
   All Liberians of this world
   Krahn, Gio, Mano and Mandingoes;
   They are precious in his sight
   Jesus loves all tribes of Liberia.

2. Jesus loves all Liberians,
   All Liberians of this world
   Congo, Via, Gola and Loma
   They are precious in his sight
   Jesus loves all Liberians in Liberia.

3. Jesus loves all Liberians,
   All Liberians of this world
   Kpellel, Belleh, Kissi and Gbadin
   They are precious in His sight
   Jesus loves all Liberians of this world.

4. Jesus loves all Liberians,
   All Liberians of this world
   Bassa, Kru, Grabo and Saapo
   They are precious in his sight
   Jesus loves all Liberians all the time.

"PRAY FOR LIBERIAN"

When you pray and I pray,
And together we pray,
The Holy Spirit will come down!
Liberia, will be saved,

Chorus// Liberia will be saved
Liberia will be saved
The Holy Spirit will come down,
Liberia will be saved! (Repeat)

"LIBERIA, WE ARE THE SONS"

1. Liberia we are the sons
   We pledge an allegiance to thee
   Liberia, the Land of our birth,
   We love you forever more,

Chorus//   In unity ever we stand
             We love you forever more
             We will be true to you,
             Liberia land that we love;

2. Liberia, our love for you
   Will forever stand for thee.
   Our hearts in Christian love,
   Will forever stand for thee.

3. Liberia, our love for liberty
   Should forever remain!
   Our quest for human freedom
   Will forever stand for all.

4. Liberians, should never fight
   Cause we are all one people,
   One nation, one destiny
   Let freedom prevail for all.

"MY COUNTRY LIBERIA"

1. My Country Liberia,
   Sweet land of liberty
   To thee I sing,
   Land where my fathers labored and die
   Land where my mother travailed for me
   From Mount Nimba to Monsurado,
   Let freedom rings!

2. My Country Liberia,
    Sweet land of liberty
    To thee I sing,
    Land where my brothers struggled for me
    Land where my sisters toiled for me
    From Cape Palms to Cape Mount
    Let freedom rise!

3. My Country Liberia,
    Sweet land of liberty
    To thee I sing,
    Land where our friends suffered for our peace
    Land where our friends laid down their lives
    From Mount Putu to Wologisi
    Let peace triumph!

4. Hair of Africa's liberty,
    The cradle of freedom,
    To thee I cry,
    Hold fast to your pride
    Preach democracy
    All over Africa
    Let Lone Star Shine!

ALL HAIL THE FLAG!

All hail the flag Red, White and Blue (Red, White and Blue)
All hail the flag Red, White and Blue (Red, White and Blue)
All hail the flag
All hail the flag
All hail the flag Red, White and Blue.

We escort our flag Red, White and Blue (Red, White and Blue
We escort our flag Red, White and Blue (Red, White and Blue)
We escort our flag
We escort our flag
We escort our flag Red, White and Blue.

We hoist our flag, Red, White and Blue (Red, White and Blue)
We hoist our flag, Red, White and Blue (Red, White and Blue)
We hoist our flag
We hoist our flag
We hoist our flag, Red, White and Blue.

We salute our flag Red, White and Blue (Red, White and Blue)
We salute our flag Red, White and Blue (Red, White and Blue)
We salute our flag
We salute our flag
We salute our flag Red, White and Blue.
Song for Kindergarten Children by Gehleigbe Bobson Bleh 2012

POEM

The flag, the flag
The flag of Liberia
It has three colors:
Red, White and Blue.

The flag, the flag
The flag of Liberia
It has eleven stripes
Six Red stripes
Five White stripes

The flag, the flag
The flag of Liberia
It has one star
White on the blue spot
Lighting the dark
Continent of Africa.

Poem for Kindergarten Children by Gehleigbe Bobson Bleh 2012

Appendix C

Some Statistical and Historical Information of Liberia*

Dispersion of Liberians during the Civil War between 1990 & 2005

Country of Residence	Time Period	Refugees and Internally Displaced People (IDP's)
Guinea	1990-2005	133,000
Cote D'Ivoire	1990-2005	65,000
Sierra Leone	1990-2005	67,000
Ghana	1990-2005	42,000
Liberia	1989-2005	500,000

*The United Nations High Commission for Refugees, UNHCR

The Distribution of Liberia's Population by County after the Civil War based on the 2008 POPULATION AND HOUSING CENSUS (LISGIS, MAY 2009)

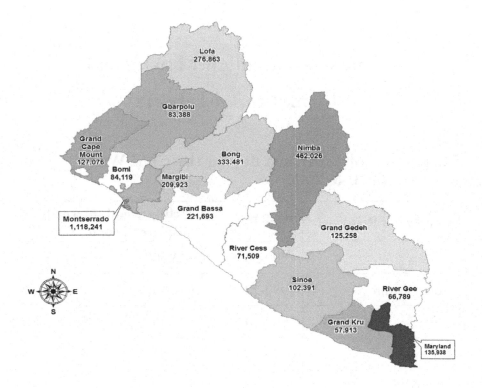

Liberia Demographics Profile 2011*

		Date
Population	3,786,764	July 2011 est.
Age structure	0-14 years: 44.3% (male 843,182/ female 834,922) 15-64 years: 52.7% (male 989,623/ female 1,007,577) 65 years and over: 2.9% (male 56,189/ female 55,271)	2011 est.
Median age	Total: 18.3 years Male: 18.2 years Female: 18.3 years	2011 est.
Population growth rate	2.663%	2011 est.
Birth rate	37.25 births/1,000 population	2011 est.
Death rate	10.62 deaths/1,000 population	July 2011 est.
Net migration rate	0 migrant(s)/1,000 population	2011 est.
Urbanization	Urban population: 48% of total population (2010) Rate of urbanization: 3.4% annual rate of change	2010-15 est.)
Sex ratio	At birth: 1.03 male(s)/female Under 15 years: 1.01 male(s)/female 15-64 years: 0.98 male(s)/female 65 years and over: 1.03 male(s)/female Total population: 1 male(s)/female	(2011 est.)
Infant mortality rate	Total: 74.52 deaths/1,000 live births Male: 78.96 deaths/1,000 live births Female: 69.95 deaths/1,000 live births (2011 est.)	(2011 est.)
Life expectancy at birth	Total population: 57 years Male: 55.44 years Female: 58.6 years (2011 est.)	
Total fertility rate	Total fertility rate 5.13 children born/woman	2011 est.

		HIV/AIDS—adult prevalence rate 1.5%	2009 est.
		HIV/AIDS—people living with HIV/AIDS 37,000	2009 est.
		HIV/AIDS—deaths 3,600	2009 est.
	Major infectious diseases	Degree of risk: very high Food or waterborne diseases: bacterial and protozoal diarrhea, hepatitis A, and typhoid fever vector borne diseases: malaria and yellow fever Water contact disease: schistosomiasis Aerosolized dust or soil contact disease: Lassa fever Animal contact disease: rabies	2009
	Ethnic groups	Kpelle 20.3%, Bassa 13.4%, Grebo 10%, Gio 8%, Mano 7.9%, Kru 6%, Lorma 5.1%, Kissi 4.8%, Gola 4.4%, other 20.1%	2008 census
	Religions	Christian 85.6%, Muslim 12.2%, Traditional 0.6%, other 0.2%, none 1.4%	2008 census
	Languages	English 20% (official), some 20 ethnic group languages few of which can be written or used in correspondence	
	Literacy	English 20% (official), some 20 ethnic group languages few of which can be written or used in correspondence School life expectancy (primary to tertiary education) Total: 11 years Male: 13 years Female: 9 years	2000
	Education expenditures	2.7% of GDP	2008
	Maternal mortality rate	990 deaths/100,000 live births	(2008)

Children under the age of 5 years underweight 20.4%)		2007
Health expenditures	3.9% of GDP)	2009
Physicians' density	0.014 physicians/1,000 population (2008) Hospital bed density 0.7 beds/1,000 population	2009

* Based on the CIA World Factbook demographic statistics for Liberia and the author does not in any way claims ownership.

Brief History of the Liberian Society*

Portuguese explorers established contacts with Liberia as early as 1461 and named the area Grain Coast because of the abundance of grains of Malegueta Pepper. In 1663 the British installed trading posts on the Grain Coast, but the Dutch destroyed these posts a year later. There were no further reports of European settlements along the Grain Coast until the arrival of freed slaves in the early 1800s.

Liberia, which means "land of the free," was founded by freed slaves from the United States in 1820. These freed slaves, called Americo-Liberians, first arrived in Liberia and established a settlement and named it, Christopolis (The City of Christ) and later changed the name to Monrovia (after U.S. President James Monroe) on February 6, 1820. This group of 86 immigrants formed the nucleus of the settler population of what became known as the Republic of Liberia.

Thousands of freed slaves from America soon arrived during the following years, leading to the formation of more settlements and culminating in a declaration of independence on July 26, 1847 of the Republic of Liberia. The idea of resettling free slaves in Africa was nurtured by the American Colonization Society (ACS), an organization that governed the

Commonwealth of Liberia until independence in 1847. The new Republic of Liberia adopted American styles of life and established thriving trade links with other West Africans.

The formation of the Republic of Liberia was not an altogether easy task. The settlers periodically encountered stiff opposition from Africans, whom they met on land upon arrival, usually resulting in bloody battles. On the other hand, the newly independent Liberia was encroached upon by colonial expansionists who forcibly took over much of the original territory of independent Liberia. The British took good portions of the Liberia on the west (Sierra Leone) while the French to take away the northern and eastern portions (Guinea and Cote D'Ivoire). If these portions were added to Liberia, the country would have been the largest country in the Mano River Basin. For instance the whole of the N'Zerekore Region (southeastern) of the Republic of Guinea should be Liberia.

Liberia's history until 1980 was mainly peaceful. For 133 years after independence, the Republic of Liberia was a one-party state ruled by the Americo-Liberian dominated True Whig Party (TWP). Joseph Jenkins Roberts, who was born and raised in America, became Liberia's first president. The style of government and constitution was fashioned on that of the United States. It is worth noting that Liberia was also a Christian nation. It was inscribed in the first constitution. The Declaration of Independence was signed in a church. It is unfortunate to note that the second constitution did not maintain the clause "Christian Nation", but was changed to "Secular Nation." The True Whig Party dominated all sectors of Liberia from independence until April 12, 1980, when indigenous Liberian Master Sergeant Samuel K. Doe—from the Krahn ethnic group, seized power in a coup d'état. Doe's forces executed President William R. Tolbert and several officials of his government, mostly of Americo-Liberian descent. As a result, 133 years of Americo-Liberian political domination ended with the formation of the People's Redemption Council (PRC).

Doe's government increasingly adopted an ethnic outlook as members of his Krahn ethnic group soon dominated political and military life in Liberia. This caused a heightened level of ethnic tension, leading to frequent hostilities between the politically and militarily dominant Krahn and other ethnic groups in the country.

Political parties remained banned until 1984. Elections were held on October 15, 1985, in which Doe's National Democratic Party of Liberia (NDPL) was declared the winner. The elections were characterized by widespread fraud and rigging. The period after the elections saw increased human rights abuses, corruption, and ethnic tensions. The standard of living, which had been rising in the 1970s, declined drastically. On November 12, 1985, former Army Commanding Gen. Thomas Quawonkpahs invaded Liberia by way of neighboring Sierra Leone and almost succeeded in toppling the government of Samuel Doe. Members of the Krahn-dominated Armed Forces of Liberia repelled Quiwonkpa's attack and executed him in Monrovia.

On December 24, 1989, a small band of rebels led by Doe's former procurement (GSA) chief, Charles Taylor, an America-Liberian, invaded Liberia from the Ivory Coast through Buotuo, a border town in Northeastern Nimba County, Liberia. Taylor and his National Patriotic Front rebels rapidly gained the support of Liberians because of the repressive nature of Samuel Doe and his government. Barely 6 six months after the rebels first attacked, had they reached the outskirts of Monrovia.

The 1989-1996 Liberian civil war, one of Africa's bloodiest, claiming the lives of more than 200,000 Liberians and further displaced a million others into refugee camps in neighboring countries. The Economic Community of West African States (ECOWAS) intervened and succeeded in preventing Charles Taylor from capturing Monrovia. Prince Johnson, who had been a member of Taylor's National Patriotic Front of Liberia (NPFL) but broke away because of policy differences, formed the Independent National Patriotic Front of Liberia (INPFL). Johnson has always asserted that Taylor did not want to uphold the original plan of the revolution. The plan was to topple the Doe's regime, set up an interim government to organize democratic elections. But Taylor declared himself as the leader of the revolution for a power grab. Johnson's forces captured and killed Doe on September 9, 1990.

An interim Government of National Unity (IGNU) was formed in Gambia under the auspices of ECOWAS in October 1990, and Dr. Amos C. Sawyer became Chairman. Taylor refused to work with the interim government and continued fighting. By 1992, several warring factions had emerged in the Liberian civil war, all of which were absorbed in the new transitional government. After several peace accords and declining military power, Taylor finally agreed to the formation of a five-man transitional government.

After considerable progress in negotiations conducted by the United States, United Nations, Organization of African Unity (now the African Union), and ECOWAS, disarmament and demobilization of warring factions were hastily carried out. Special elections were held on July 19, 1997, with Charles Taylor and his National Patriotic Party emerging victorious. One of the unfortunate statements ever made by Liberians,

"You killed my pa, you killed my ma, I will vote for you," was Taylor's campaign slogan. He won the election by a large majority, primarily because Liberians feared a return to war had Taylor lost. Secondly, the security of the nation was in the hands of Taylor. Thirdly, the people were ignorant in that there was no concrete voter education.

For the next six years, the Taylor government did not improve the lives of Liberians. Unemployment and illiteracy stood above 75%, and little investment was made in the country's infrastructure. Liberia is still trying to recover from the ravages of war; six years after the war, pipe-borne water and electricity were still unavailable, and schools, hospitals, roads, and infrastructure remained derelict. Rather than work to improve the lives of Liberians, Taylor supported the bloody Revolutionary United Front in Sierra Leone, fomenting unrest and brutal excesses in the region, and leading to the resumption of armed rebellion from among Taylor's former adversaries.

On June 4, 2003 in Accra, Ghana, ECOWAS facilitated the inauguration of peace talks among the Government of Liberia, civil society, and the rebel groups called "Liberians United for Reconciliation and Democracy" (LURD) and "Movement for Democracy in Liberia" (MODEL). LURD and MODEL largely represented elements of the former ULIMO-K (organized by A. V. Kromah of the Mandingo ethnic group) and ULIMO-J (Roosevelt Johnson of the Krahn ethnic group) factions that fought Taylor during Liberia's previous civil war (1989-1996). Also on June 4, 2003 the Chief Prosecutor of the Special Court for Sierra Leone issued a press statement announcing the indictment of Liberian President Charles Taylor for "bearing the greatest responsibility" for atrocities in Sierra Leone since November 1996. By July 17, 2003 the Government of Liberia, LURD, and MODEL signed a cease-fire that envisioned a comprehensive peace agreement within 30 days. The three combatants subsequently broke that cease-fire repeatedly, which resulted in bitter fighting that eventually reached downtown Monrovia.

On August 11, 2003 under intense U.S. and international pressure, President Taylor resigned office and departed into exile in Nigeria. This move paved the way for the deployment by ECOWAS of what became a 3,600-strong peacekeeping mission in Liberia (ECOMIL). The transition to the interim government was led by the Vice President of Taylor, Moses Z. Blah, who had been a top general in the Taylor's NPFL. The United States provided limited direct military support and $26 million in logistical assistance to ECOMIL and another $40 million in humanitarian assistance to Liberia. On August 18, leaders from the Liberian Government, the rebels, political parties, and civil society signed a comprehensive peace agreement that laid the framework for constructing a 2-year National Transitional Government of Liberia, effective October 14. On August 21, they selected businessman Gyude Bryant as Chair and Wesley Johnson as Vice Chair of the National Transitional Government of Liberia (NTGL). Under the terms of the agreement the LURD, MODEL, and Government of Liberia each selected 12 members of the 76-member Legislative Assembly (LA). The NTGL was inducted on October 14, 2003 and served until January 2006, when Madam Ellen Johnson Sirleaf and the winners of the October 2005 presidential and congressional elections took office. ECOMIL was succeeded by a new international force, United Mission in Liberia (UMIL). UMIL has since been working and monitoring the Comprehensive Peace Agreement (CPA).

In 2005, Madam Ellen Johnson Sirleaf won the Presidential elections, resulting in her historic inauguration, on January 16, 2006, as the first female President of Liberia. President Ellen Johnson Sirleaf has devoted time in rebuilding post-conflict Liberia. She has revived national hope by strengthening the institutions of national security and good governance. She has led the revitalization of the national economy and infrastructure, including the construction of more than 800 miles of roads. She has restored Liberia's international reputation and credibility, thereby building strong relations with regional partners and the international community. On January 16, 2012, Madam Sirleaf was inaugurated for her second term as the 24th President of the Republic of Liberia. In her inaugural address she assured the Liberians of continuing what she began doing in the first term of her presidency. Liberians and the international community has rated President Sirleaf as the most democratic president because of her respect for the rule of law, press freedom and the reduction of poverty. She along with Laymah (Lemah Gbowee and Tawakul Karman of Yamen received the 2011 Nobel Peace Prize.

*This article is found at www. http://en.wikipedia.org/wiki/History of Liberia and the author does not in any way claims ownership.

BIBLIOGRAPHY

Adjei, Manuel, Lecture Notes on the fifty century
Post-Exilic prophet Haggai: Ghana Christian Collage and Seminary,
    Abeka, Accra, Ghana, 1995.

Anderson, B. The Eighth Century Prophet, Amos, Hosea, Isaiah and
    Micah, SPCK, 1978.

Alexander, Pat and David. Ed, The Lion Handbook
    To the Bible.
    Lion Publishing House, Grand Rapids,

Barker, Kenneth, Ed. The NIV Study Bible.
    Zondervan Publishing House, Grand Rapids,
    MI, USA, 1995.

Kulah, Arthur F. Liberia Will Rise Again.
    Abingdon Press, Nashville, U.S.A, 1999.

Rad, Gerhard Von. The Message of The Prophet. London, c 1979.

Robinson, Theodore. Prophecy and the Prophets in ancient Israel,
    Duckworth, c 1979.

VanGemeren, William A. <u>Interpreting the Prophetic Word</u>: an Introduction to Prophetic Literature of the Old Testament, Grand Rapids, MI: Zondervan, 1996.

Wood, Leon. <u>A Survey of Israel's History</u>. Grand Rapids, Zondervan, c 1970.

_____ The <u>Prophets of Israel</u>. Grand Rapids: Baker Book House, c 1979.

Zodhiates, Spiros. <u>The Hebrew-Greek key study Bible</u>.
(New American Standard Version):
AMG Publishers Chattanooga, TN
U.S.A 190.

* Unpublished.

ABOUT THE AUTHOR

The author is a native of Yarsonnoh, a town in Nimba County, Liberia, West Africa. He was born in the mining town of Yekepa, to Joseph Sei-Tohemehn and Woryenuah Marie Bleh. He accepted Jesus Christ as his personal Lord and Savior when Pastor Borbor K. Dolo of the Mid Baptist Church preached to him and other students during his primary school at the Duo Public School (1983). He completed his Junior High School education at the John Wesley Pearson Junior High School (1988) and subsequently enrolled at the Ganta United Methodist Senior High school (GUMS) in March 1989. He was awarded work grant scholarship by the school to enable him complete his studies. In 1990 Bobson was forced to flee to the Ivory Coast due to the Liberian Civil War. As refuge, he continued his education at the Protestant Methodist Resources Center organized by United Methodist missionaries, Herbert and Mary Zigbuo, who were heads of the Ganta United Methodist School. The center was sponsored by the Operation Classroom of Indiana USA, for the education of Liberian refugees. On March 29, 1993, Bobson completed his high school studies and subsequently in September of the same year enrolled at the Ghana Christian University College (formerly Ghana Christian College and Seminary) and graduated in 1996. He returned to the Ivory Coast and later Liberia, where he taught at his Alma meter, the Ganta United Methodist School (1997-2002). In 2002, Bobson returned to Ghana where he earned Master of Art degree in Adult Education from the Wisconsin International University College, Ghana.

Bobson is an ordained elder in the Liberian Annual Conference of the United Methodist Church. He took his first pastoral appointment at the Miller McAllister UMC, where he served as associate Pastor for four years. He also served the Gompa District as District Evangelist, where he planted churches and revitalized over forty congregations and structured them into eight pastoral Areas or circuits.

Bobson also served as instructor for Bible and Religious Education at the Ganta United Methodist School and the Winifred J. Harley College of Health Sciences, United Methodist University (UMU). He served as senior pastor of the First United Methodist Church in Sanniquellie, Nimba County (2002). In 2004 Bobson was the Evangelist appointed to the United Methodist Church Ministry at the Buduburam United Methodist Church in Ghana. He planted a church in Kasoa, a commercial Town outside Accra, on the Accra-Winneba motorway.

From 2005-2011, Bobson served as the Supervising Pastor of the Guinea Ministry of the United Methodist Church, Republic of Guinea, West Africa; where He supervised the affairs of over ten congregations.

Bobson works with his conference board of ordained ministry as the Chairman for the Gompa District Committee ordained Ministry, Liberia Annual Conference of the United Methodist Church. Bobson has traveled and preached in three West African Countries: Ivory Coast, Guinea and Ghana. His mission is to evangelize the indigenous in West Africa and beyond as the Lord leads.

He is married to Susannah Paye-Tee Bleh and this union is blessed with three beautiful girls: Marthalene Kou-Walakewon, Thalee Sue Grace, and Caroline Lorkeak.

Bobson and his family currently live in Yekepa, his birth city, where he serves as the Senior Pastor of the Yekepa United Methodist Church and Professor at the ABC University. He is the founder and proprietor of the Marth-Carol International Day Care School which provides early childhood education and care for kids in the Yekepa Community. He is currently the President of the Yekepa Evangelical Christian Fellowship (formerly Yekepa Pastoral Fellowship), a local body of Evangelical Churches in Yekepa.